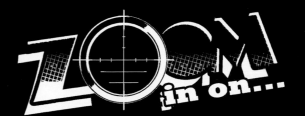

BIZARRE
BUGS

Richard Spilsbury

Enslow Publishers, Inc.
40 Industrial Road
Box 398
Berkeley Heights, NJ 07922
USA

http://www.enslow.com

This edition published by Enslow Publishers Inc.

Library of Congress Cataloging-in-Publication Data:

Spilsbury, Richard, 1963–
  Zoom in on bizarre bugs / Richard Spilsbury.
    p. cm. — (Zoom in on—)
  Summary: "Read about weird and unusual bugs, and see close up images of them"—Provided by publisher.
  ISBN 978-0-7660-4309-1
  1. Insects–Juvenile literature. I. Title. II. Series: Spilsbury, Richard, 1963– Zoom in on—
  QL467.2.S74 2013
  595.7–dc23
                              2012045281
Future editions:
Paperback ISBN: 978-1-4644-0563-1

To Our Readers:
We have done our best to make sure all Internet addresses in this book were active and appropriate when we went to press. However, the author and the publisher have no control over and assume no liability for the material available on those Internet sites or on other Web sites they may link to. Any comments or suggestions can be sent by e-mail to comments@enslow.com or to the address on the back cover.

Printed in China

122012 WKT, Shenzhen, Guangdong, China

10 9 8 7 6 5 4 3 2 1

First published in the UK in 2012 by Wayland

Copyright © Wayland 2012

Wayland
338 Euston Rd
London NW1 3BH

Commissioning editor: Victoria Brooker
Project editor: Alice Harman
Designer: Paul Cherrill for Basement68
Picture research: Richard Spilsbury and Alice Harman
Proofreader and indexer: Martyn Oliver
Produced for Wayland by
White-Thomson Publishing Ltd

www.wtpub.co.uk

Wayland is a division of Hachette Children's Books,

an Hachette UK company.

www.hachette.co.uk

Picture Credits: 3, 8, Dreamstime/Steveheap; 3, 12 (top), Shutterstock/ Dr. Morley Read; 4, 11 (bottom), Shutterstock/ kurt_G; 5, 20 Dreamstime/Andrey Bolovintsev; 6, Alamy/The Natural History Museum; 7 (top), Dreamstime/Kadmy; 7 (bottom), Dreamstime/cpdp; 9 (top), Science Photo Library/David Scharf; 9 (bottom), Dreamstime/Orionmystery; 10 (left), Dreamstime/ Vladimir Blinov; 10 (right), 29, Dreamstime/Lochef; 11 (top), Science Photo Library/John Walsh; 12 (bottom), Shutterstock/Dr. Morley Read; 13, Dreamstime/Ryszard Laskowski; 14 Dreamstime/Neal Cooper; 15, Alamy/Xunbin Pan; 16, Science Photo Library/Brian Brake; 17, Dreamstime/Cathy Keifer; 18, Alamy/Jonathan Plant; 19, Science Photo Library/Wim Van Egmond, Visuals Unlimited; 20, Dreamstime/Andrey Bolovintsev; 21, Science Photo Library/Steve Gschmeissner; 22, 28, Dreamstime/Dleonis; 23, Science Photo Library/Claude Nuridsany & Marie Perennou; 25 (top), Science Photo Library/Lawrence Lawry; 25 (bottom), Shutterstock/Rob Byron; 26, Wikimedia/Aiwok; 27 (top), 30, Dreamstime/Mike Rogal; 27 (bottom), Wikimedia/Aiwok; cover, Science Photo Library/Power and Syred.

CONTENTS

The scale of things   6

Assassin bugs   8

Hovering hunters   10

Army ant march   12

Dining on dung   14

Flashing fireflies   16

Armed earwigs   18

Ladybugs fight back   20

Swarming locusts   22

The hug of death   24

Parasites bursting out   26

Glossary   28

Find out more   29

Index   30

THE SCALE OF THINGS

About half of all the types of animals on Earth are insects. Many use fascinating special features or adaptations to survive, but these are not easy to see. Scientists use powerful microscopes to zoom in on these bizarre bugs and study them.

Invisible world

It's hard to imagine how small some things really are. The smallest objects the human eye can see are about 0.2 mm long. There are 1000 **microns** to a millimeter. A human hair (with a width of about 100 microns) is vast, compared to most things scientists zoom in on!

Sense of scale

A scale tells you how big something is, compared to its real size. When an image is said to be 25x, that means it's 25 times larger than actual size. You'll see scales next to many images in this book, to give you a sense of the size of objects.

This butterfly is
50 TIMES
its actual size

The coiled tube on a butterfly's head is its **proboscis**. The butterfly uncoils its proboscis to poke deep into flowers and suck sweet **nectar**.

Adapt to survive

Animals can only survive if they eat and avoid being eaten by others. Many of the bizarre bugs in this book have adaptations—special body parts or behaviors—to help them catch prey and defend against attack by predators. Others have adaptations to help find mates, so they can produce young.

Tools of the trade

How can we zoom in on things? Light **microscopes** bounce light off surfaces to create images. They use lenses (curved pieces of glass) that bend light rays to **magnify** an image. The most powerful light microscopes can magnify things up to about 2000 times!

A light microscope.

Scanning electron microscopes (SEMs)

These microscopes use electrons instead of light. (Electrons are tiny parts inside **atoms**.) SEMs bounce electrons off surfaces to create images. Electron microscopes can magnify things by almost a million times!

Birds and other predators love to eat bugs, however bizarre they look!

7

ASSASSIN BUGS

Assassin bugs got their creepy name because they silently hide and wait to attack other insects that pass by. Then they kill them with a dagger-like weapon!

Stabbed in the dark

Assassin bugs hunt at night, under the cover of darkness. They stab flies, beetles, and other **prey** with their long proboscis. Then they suck out their victims' blood or insides! Assassin bugs mostly hunt other insects. Some feed on the blood of birds and other animals, including humans. Sometimes, they even eat each other!

When a deadly assassin bug stabs its prey, there is no escape!

Fearsome fact

Some assassin bugs pluck spiders' webs to make them think a fly is trapped, then eat the spiders when they get close!

Kissing bugs

In Central and South America, some types of assassin bugs are known as kissing bugs. They got this name because they often bite people near the mouth while they are sleeping. Yuck!

8

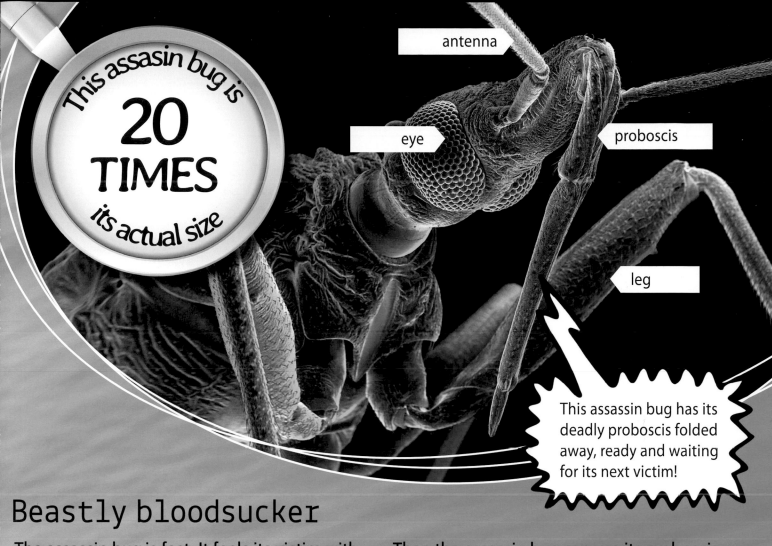

antenna

eye

proboscis

leg

This assassin bug has its deadly proboscis folded away, ready and waiting for its next victim!

Beastly bloodsucker

The assassin bug is fast. It feels its victim with its long, thin **antennae**, then swiftly stabs with its sharp proboscis. This proboscis injects the unlucky prey with a deadly poison. This **paralyzes** the insect and stops it from moving. The poison also turns the insect's insides into liquid.

Then the assassin bug can use its proboscis to suck up this soupy substance. When the assassin bug has sucked its victim dry, it folds the proboscis under its head... and waits to strike again!

The assassin bug uses its dagger-like proboscis to suck other insects dry!

KNOW YOUR FOE

Gardeners like assassin bugs, because they eat other bugs that might eat and damage plants. But people must be careful not to touch assassin bugs. They can easily puncture your skin too!

HOVERING HUNTERS

Dragonflies are the helicopters of the bug world! They can dart through the sky at up to 48 km (30 miles) an hour, swerving swiftly, stopping suddenly, and hovering in midair.

Spotting lunch

Dragonflies move fast and perform acrobatics in the sky because they hunt other flying insects. At the top of their long, thin bodies are two eyes so big they cover most of the head! These huge eyes help a dragonfly to spot other insects from as far as 6 m (20 ft) away.

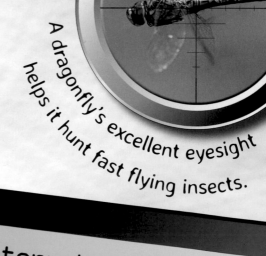

A dragonfly's excellent eyesight helps it hunt fast flying insects.

An adult dragonfly coming out of its **larva** skin.

Fearsome fact

Dragonflies have six legs (like all insects), but they only use them to perch on plants. They cannot walk!

Watery beginnings

Dragonflies start life underwater. Larvae hatch from eggs and swim around eating tadpoles and underwater insects. After several years, the larvae crawl out of the water and become adults.

Eye spy

Humans have two eyes, but dragonflies have the equivalent of 30,000! Dragonflies have two **compound eyes**. Each eye is made up of thousands of tiny **facets**. Each facet collects light and sends messages to the brain. Each facet points a slightly different way, so dragonflies can see in all directions at the same time. Compound eyes wrap around a dragonfly's head, so it can watch insects fly overhead.

Thousands of facets fit together perfectly to make a compound eye.

Dragonflies have bigger compound eyes than any other insect.

This dragonfly is **20 TIMES** its actual size

11

ARMY ANT MARCH

Army ants are the ultimate fighting force. They march in long, neat lines called columns, capturing and eating any insects, spiders, and other animals they find on the way. There are more than 300 types of army ant worldwide, and most live in the rainforests of Africa,

An army ant carries a larva to a new camp.

Unstoppable!

Army ants usually live in colonies of around 1 million. Most types of ants prefer to sneak around, but army ants march where they can be easily seen. A typical colony of army ants can eat around 100,000 insects and other minibeasts in a day! Nothing stops them. If there is a gap in their path, some of the ants form a bridge that the other ants climb over.

Army ants cling to each other to make a bridge.

Baby on board

Army ants are always on the move, and any young ants still in larvae form must be carried. So, some of the adult ants link together using hooks and spines on their feet and their mouths. They make a living nest from their own bodies!

A soldier ant ready to attack!

This ant is **22 TIMES** its actual size

Weapons of war

As in a human army, army ants have different ranks. The queen is the leader. She lays eggs and stays with the larvae that hatch out. Worker ants do the work. Some make nests, while some guard the queen and the other ants from animals that attack the colony.

Soldier ants catch, cut up, and carry prey back to the nest. They have large heads and huge, curving **mandibles**. They use these scissor-like jaws for crushing, cutting, and biting.

KNOW YOUR FOE

All army worker ants are blind, so they leave chemical trails on the ground. These act as indicators to help them find their way and follow each other. The ants' antennas detect the trails.

Fearsome fact

Some big army ant colonies contain 1.5 million individuals. When they march, they form a line over 1,600 feet long!

DINING ON DUNG

Imagine having dung for dinner. Not pizza, pasta, or peas – dung! That's what dung beetles eat, which is how they got their name. Dung beetles live all over the world and eat all sorts of dung, or poo.

Dung for dinner

Some dung beetles dig under dung heaps and drag dung into their tunnels. Other dung beetles shape dung into balls and roll it away before they eat it. Some dung beetles live inside dung and eat it from the inside out! Most dung beetles use their sense of smell to find animal dung. Some hitch a ride on an animal until it produces dung, then drop off to eat this warm, fresh dinner.

Some dung beetles try to steal other beetles' dung balls rather than make their own!

Fearsome fact

Dung beetles live all over the world, on every continent except Antarctica!

14

Born into dung

Some dung beetles lay their eggs in dung balls. When larvae hatch out of the eggs, they feed on the dung and grow into adult beetles.

Dung duty

Dung beetles are only 1 cm to 6 cm long (0.4 to 2.4 inches), but they are very strong. Most can roll a ball of dung 50 times heavier than they are! Close-up, you can see other features that help them do their job.

Their head is flat and wide so they can use it like a shovel to scrape and push balls of dung. They have hard wing cases that they can tuck their wings under for protection when digging. The tough spines on their legs help them to dig and to drag dung balls over the ground.

Dung beetles can eat their own weight of dung in a day!

wing case

wing

leg

spines

KNOW YOUR FOE

Without dung beetles, many places would be covered in dung! Dung beetles get rid of waste that could attract flies and spread disease. By breaking down the waste they also help to enrich the soil.

This dung beetle is **10 TIMES** its actual size

FLASHING FIREFLIES

Have you ever seen mysterious, tiny lights flashing on a tree at night, or on the walls of a dark cave? This is the work of fireflies, also known as lightning bugs. Fireflies are beetles that produce light to send messages to each other.

Look at me

Fireflies mostly put on their light shows to attract other fireflies. A male firefly flashes a pattern of light as he flies around. Females wait on trees, bushes, grass, or cave walls to find a male. If one is impressed by his light signal, she signals back to call him over.

Sometimes lots of fireflies flash lights at the same time and in the same pattern—kind of like a silent disco!

Turn off those lights!

There are fewer fireflies than in the past because of electric lights. Bright lights at night stop fireflies from noticing others' light signals. This means they cannot find each other to mate and produce young.

Light factory

Fireflies make light in their **abdomen**. **Cells** here contain two chemicals called luciferin and luciferase. The cells keep the chemicals separate until the time when the firefly needs to light up. Then the chemicals mix, and the luciferin glows!

This firefly is **10 TIMES** its actual size

Fireflies are about half the length of a paperclip.

KNOW YOUR FOE

Some types of fireflies are sneaky. They flash light patterns that copy those made by females of different types of fireflies. When males come close to investigate, they eat them!

Fearsome fact

Firefly larvae glow all the time. The light is a message to **predators** that they taste unpleasant.

ARMED EARWIGS

Earwigs are flat insects that toads and birds love to eat. They mostly keep out of sight by squeezing under rocks or plants. But when they are spotted, they have several weapons at the ready to defend themselves.

Back off!

An earwig's main defence is the set of hard pinchers at the end of its abdomen. These can give predators a nasty nip. Some earwigs can spray a smelly liquid from their bottoms up to 10 cm (4 inches), to put off predators!

pinchers

wing covers

Marvelous mothers

Female earwigs are very protective of their eggs and young. They clean and stack their eggs to stop them from going moldy. Females collect food for the young, and defend them from spiders and other attackers.

antennas

Earwigs arch up their abdomen to face their weapons forward.

Earwig multi-tool

Few explorers would go into the wild without a multi-tool for different tasks. An earwig's pinchers are like a multi-tool. They are good grippers. Earwigs use them to hold prey while they feed and other earwigs while they mate! Pinchers also help earwigs to fold up their wings. The pinchers are hard and tough, yet sensitive enough to feel slight air movements and noises. This tells earwigs if predators or prey are around.

Muscles in the earwig's abdomen pull their two pinchers together like tweezers.

LADYBUGS FIGHT BACK

Ladybugs are small and pretty beetles, but they know how to handle themselves in a fight. They have several forms of defense. Can you guess how their knees come in handy?

Under attack

Some birds and insects eat small beetles like ladybugs. If a ladybug is attacked, it squeezes a smelly yellow liquid out of its knees. This is blood. The blood can stain things, and it tastes really nasty. After a bird has tasted this, it won't try to eat another ladybug.

Warning signals

Ladybugs are not bright and colorful so that they look pretty in your garden. Their black and red pattern helps to protect them. It's a warning signal to birds that they taste bad, so that the birds don't try to eat them.

aphid

Ladybugs eat small insects like these black aphids.

Fearsome fact

A ladybug lives for around one year and can eat 5,000 aphids in this time!

Ladybug legs

Ladybugs also have a small pair of claws at the end of each leg. They use these to grip surfaces, so that they can walk up plants and even walk upside down!

Ladybugs also use their legs to clean themselves. Close up, you can also see the jaws and palps. The jaws catch small insects, and the palps taste the insects and push them into the mouth.

Up close, you can see a ladybug's knees and mouthparts beneath its shell.

head

palps

jaws

knee

This ladybug is **80 TIMES** its actual size

KNOW YOUR FOE

Ladybugs come in different colors. In some countries there are blue and orange or bright pink ladybugs! Ladybugs also have different numbers of spots, from 2 to 24. Count them next time you see a ladybug!

SWARMING LOCUSTS

A swarm of locusts can contain so many insects that it blocks out the sun! This huge group of locusts flies and eats quickly. It can completely destroy every plant that gets in its way.

Greedy grass-eaters

Locusts are a type of grasshopper. They use their long back legs like a catapult to help them jump between plants. A locust can leap up to 20 times the length of its own body. Locusts fly up to 80 km (50 miles) a day to find food. Swarms of feeding locusts leave behind poisonous poo. Layers of their poo can be several inches deep, and they ruin any plants the insects missed!

Locusts can eat their own weight in food every day.

Fearsome fact

Spiders, birds, and foxes eat locusts. Some greedy birds eat so many that they become too heavy to take off!

Stopping swarms

In places like Australia, locust swarms destroy entire fields of crops. This is a disaster for farmers. In summer, spotter planes fly about looking for locust swarms. When they find one, another plane sprays chemicals that kill the greedy pests.

Alien insect?

Up close, a locust's face looks like something from a horror film! The locust's mouth is made up of several parts. The lip-like parts are called labra, and they are hard rather than soft. They help to cut leaves and to taste them. The powerful mandibles bite or saw off pieces of leaf, and grind them up. The fingerlike palps that hang down at either side of the mouth taste food. They check if it is safe and good to eat.

This locust is **10 TIMES** its actual size

antenna

eye

A locust's mouth is designed to make it an eating machine!

KNOW YOUR FOE

A single swarm of locusts can contain 10,000 million locusts. A large swarm may eat 160,000 tons of a plant like corn each day. That would feed 800,000 people for a whole year!

labrum

palp

THE HUG OF DEATH

The praying mantis got its name because when it bends its huge front legs together, it looks like it is praying! But this insect is not peaceful. It uses its legs to catch insects in a deadly embrace.

No escape!

A praying mantis eats live animals like crickets, grasshoppers, flies, and other insects. It stays hidden to catch them, or follows them slowly. When it's time to pounce, the praying mantis snaps its huge front legs around its victim. The legs grip the insects tightly, while the praying mantis eats them... head first!

A hug from a praying mantis is deadly for an insect!

Fearsome fact

The female praying mantis often eats the male just after mating!

KNOW YOUR FOE

Close up, the praying mantis looks like something from another planet! It has huge compound eyes on top of a triangle-shaped head. The head can turn 180 degrees to help it spot prey.

This praying mantis is

40 TIMES

its actual size

spike

leg

The spikes of a praying mantis leg close together like a metal trap!

A spiked trap

The front legs of a praying mantis are very strong, and have a secret weapon. They are lined with hard, very sharp spikes. So when a praying mantis wraps its legs around an insect, the spikes on the upper and lower legs press into the insect's body. These spiky legs can slice an insect in half! This happens very quickly. The legs snap together in just one-twentieth of a second.

Clever camouflage

When a praying mantis sits still, it is almost invisible! Most of these insects are green or brown and they are shaped like branches, leaves, or stems.

25

PARASITES BURSTING OUT

Female stylops parasites spend their entire lives inside other insects, from bees to cockroaches. These bodies provide food and a safe place for the parasites to raise their young.

Opposites attract

The female stylops is never seen fully out in the open. She has no wings or legs, and lives in a space within a bee's abdomen until she is ready to mate. Then she bursts through the bee's body and produces a special scent. The male is a tiny fly with googly eyes and crumpled wings. These give this animal its common name—the twisted-wing parasite. The male uses his antler-shaped antennas to smell her out!

Fearsome fact

Males have unusual blackberry-shaped eyes, like those found on **fossil** sea creatures called trilobites!

The male stylops lives for just five days. In that time, his only task is to mate with a female living in a bee!

From bee to bee

The stylops eggs hatch into larvae inside their mother. They then spill out of the bee through the female's head. The larvae climb onto another bee and produce chemicals that dissolve a hole in its abdomen. They squeeze inside and start to feed on the bee's blood and insides. Some develop into new females, and others into males that fly away.

Bursting out! The yellow dots on this bee's abdomen are female stylops poking out, waiting to mate with passing males.

Stylops larvae can easily pass from one bee to another in a tightly packed beehive.

Puppet master

A female stylops makes her bee host behave how she wants it to. A chemical she makes forces the bee to rush around faster than usual from flower to flower. Larvae spread onto more flowers and infect more new bees!

This strepsipteran is **20 TIMES** its actual size

27

GLOSSARY

abdomen rear section of an insect's body

antennas sensitive, jointed parts that insects use to smell and feel

assassin a killer who murders his or her victim in a surprise attack

atom one of the tiny particles that make up everything in the world

camouflage color and shape that helps an organism hide from predators or prey

cell the smallest, most basic unit from which all living things are made

compound eye type of eye found in most insects, made up of several independent light-sensing parts

facet individual part in a compound eye

fossil remains (or imprint) of a plant or animal that lived a very long time ago

larvae young hatched from eggs of certain types of animals, including insects, fish, and frogs

magnify to make bigger, enlarge

mandibles tough mouthparts of insects, used mostly as jaws to cut or crush food

micron unit of measurement equal to one-millionth of a meter; 12 microns is about half the width of a human hair

microscope device that produces enlarged images of objects that are normally too small to be seen

nectar sweet liquid produced by flowers to attract animals that help them to make seeds

paralyze to stop something from moving or feeling

parasite living thing that uses another to feed or otherwise benefit, usually harming the host (the living thing it uses) in the process

predator animal that hunts others to eat

prey animal that is hunted and eaten by others

proboscis long, usually tube-like mouthpart that insects can use for sucking up food

FIND OUT MORE

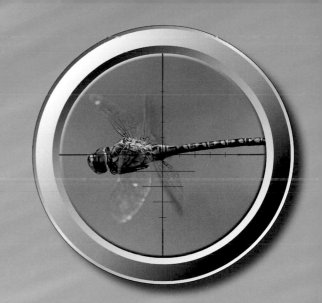

Books

Insect Investigators: Entomologists (Scientists at work)
  by Richard and Louise Spilsbury (Heinemann, 2008)

Insects (DK Handbooks) by George C. McGavin
  (Dorling Kindersley, 2010)

Extraordinary Bugs by Leon Gray (Wayland, 2011)

Up Close: Micro Bugs by Paul Harrison (Watts, 2011)

The World of the Microscope (Usborne Science and Experiments)
  by Chris Oxlade and Corinne Stockley (Usborne, 2008)

Websites

Have you ever thought of studying insects for a living? You can read an interview
with an entomologist at <www.nhm.ac.uk/kids-only/ologist/entomologist>

Did you know that some people around the world eat insects?
Find out more at <www.ca.uky.edu/entomology/dept/bugfood2.asp>

If eating bugs is not to your taste, then what about keeping insects as pets?
Useful information can be found at <www.amentsoc.org/insects/caresheets>
and <http://www.uky.edu/Ag/CritterFiles/casefile/casefile.htm>

This book only covers a small range of bugs, but you can see many
more at <www.uky.edu/Ag/CritterFiles/casefile/casefile.htm>
and <www.amentsoc.org/insects/fact-files/a-to-z-of-insects.html>. The second website
has a fascinating section on bees and wasps, including the spider-hunting wasp!

Would you like to have live access to a scanning electron microscope to look at
insects you find? Go to <bugscope.beckman.uiuc.edu> and ask a parent, teacher, or a
responsible adult to help you sign up for the program.

INDEX

antennas 9, 13, 18, 23, 26
aphid 20
army ant 12–13
assassin bug 8–9

bee 26, 27
beetle 6, 8, 14, 15, 16, 20
birds 7, 8, 18, 20, 22
blood 8, 20, 27

camouflage 25
chemicals 13, 17, 22
claws 21
cockroach 26
colony 12, 13
compound eye 11, 24

defense 18, 20
dragonfly 10–11
dung beetle 14–15

earwig 18–19
eggs 10, 13, 14, 18, 27
eye 6, 8, 10, 11, 23, 24, 26

firefly 16–17

grasshopper 22, 24

jaws 13, 21

ladybug 20–21
larvae 10, 12, 13, 14, 17, 26
legs 9, 10, 15, 21, 22, 24, 25, 26
light microscope 7
locust 22–23

mandibles 13, 23
microscope 6, 7
mouthparts 13, 21, 23

nectar 6
nest 12, 13

palps 21, 23
parasite 26, 27
pinchers 18, 19
poison 9, 22
praying mantis 24–25
predator 7, 17, 18, 19

prey 7, 8, 9, 13, 19, 24
proboscis 6, 8, 9

queen ant 13

rainforest 12

scanning electron microscope (SEM) 7
shell 21
spider 8, 12, 18, 22
stylops 26–27
swarm 22, 23

weapons 8, 9, 18, 25
wings 15, 18, 19, 26

young 7, 12, 16, 18, 26

Zoom In On...

Contents of titles in the series

Zoom in on Bizarre Bugs

978-0-7660-4309-1
The scale of things
Assassin bugs
Hovering hunters
Army ant march
Dining on dung
Flashing fireflies
Armed earwigs
Ladybugs fight back
Swarming locusts
The hug of death
Parasites bursting out
Glossary
Find out more
Index

Zoom in on Crime Scenes

978-0-7660-4311-4
The scale of things
Unique fingerprints
Hairy hints
Secret cells
Glassy giveaways
Details in the dust
How plants help police
Suspect soil
Watery grave
Maggot attack
Close to the bone
Glossary
Find out more
Index

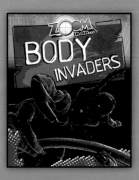

Zoom in on Body Invaders

978-0-7660-4310-7
The scale of things
Bed bugs get biting
Lice on the loose
Eyelash bugs
Hop aboard the Flea Express
Ticks latch on
Gut-squatting worms
Tooth attack
Mosquito hijackers
Worms under the skin
Viruses hitch a ride
Glossary
Find out more
Index

Zoom in on House of Horrors

978-0-7660-4312-1
The scale of things
Moldy old food
Nasty housefly habits
Creepy cockroaches
Spinning spiders
Carpet creatures
Skin-devouring mites
Paper-munching silverfish
Nasty wasp nests
Wiggly woodworms
Termite invaders
Glossary
Find out more
Index